The Rainbow Feelings of Cancer

A Book for Children Who Have a Loved One with Cancer

CARRIE MARTIN AND CHIA MARTIN

ILLUSTRATIONS BY CARRIE MARTIN

HOHM PRESS • CHINO VALLEY, ARIZONA

Self-portrait with purple hair, age 6

ISBN: 978-1-942493-13-6

HOHM PRESS
P.O. Box 4410
Chino Valley, AZ 86323
1-800-381-2700
www.hohmpress.com

To all parents and children
who have stood beneath this rainbow.

An Update from Carrie

When I was twelve, my mom passed away.
After my mom died, my feelings of sadness and anger became stronger.
My mom taught me that feelings are a part of life.
My mom showed me that for every bad experience I have, I will also have a good experience; for every time I am sad, there will be another time I am happy.
I will always be sad that she is not here; however, more than anything else, I will always feel grateful for the time I had with her, and for all the things she taught me.

My dad was diagnosed with cancer when I was seventeen.
The feelings I experienced were the same as when my mom was diagnosed, only less scary because I was familiar with these feelings.
My dad passed away when I was twenty years old.
My dad taught me to keep the people I love close to my heart.
My dad showed me how to listen to what people need, and how to help other people when they are in need of it.

I am now twenty-five years old.
Last year I moved to Boston to attend Simmons College.
I am studying to become a Social Worker.
My mom and dad taught me that I can have a life filled with happiness, compassion and love.
I wish the same for you.

Chia's Note

Creating this book was one of the best things Carrie and I ever did together.
It unfolded because we both needed it.
I hope it can serve as an inspiration for you, whether or not your lives have been touched by cancer.

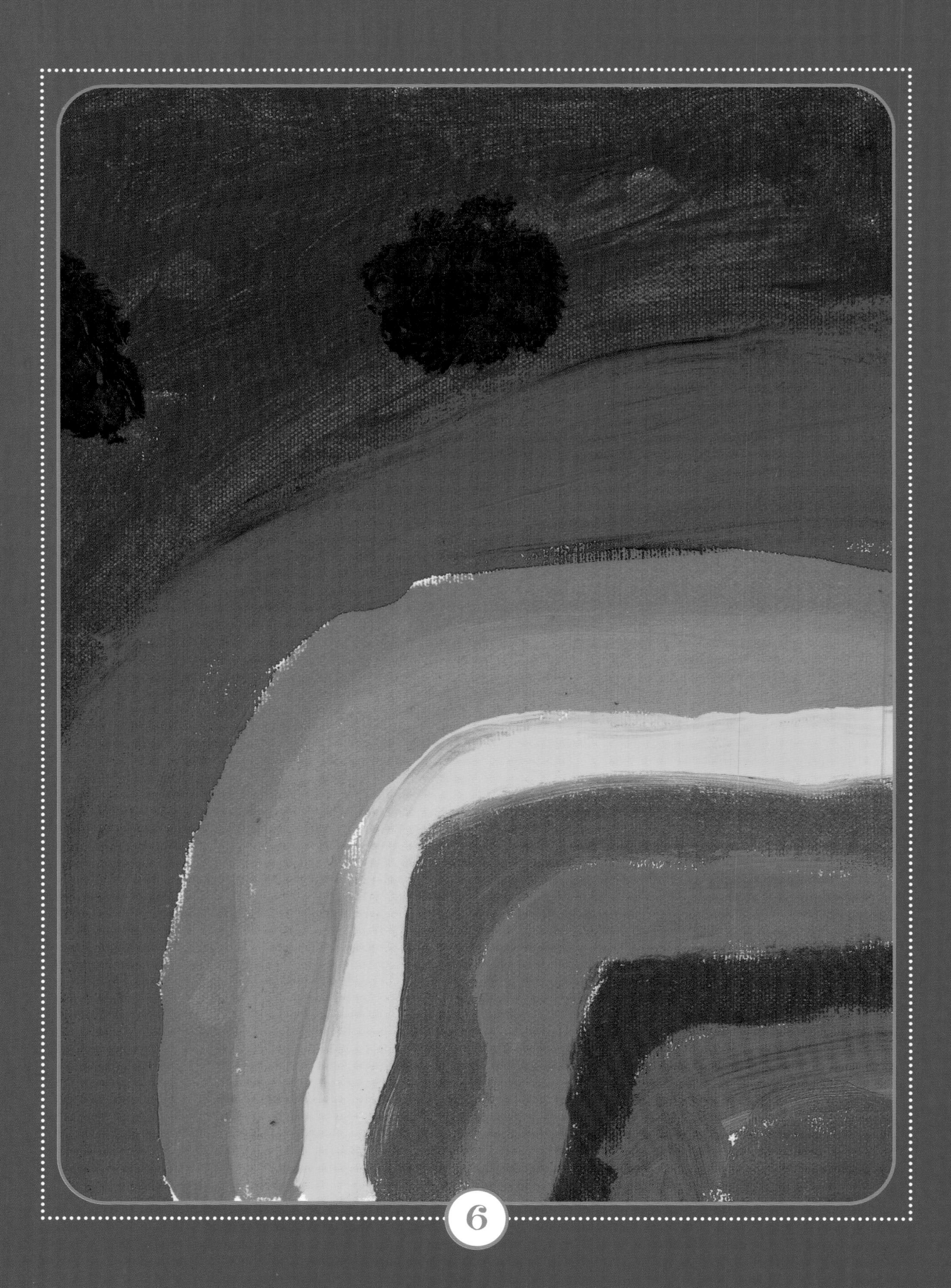

First, I want to say one thing about rainbows.

Have you ever noticed that a rainbow sky is usually blue and clear on one side and black and stormy on the other?

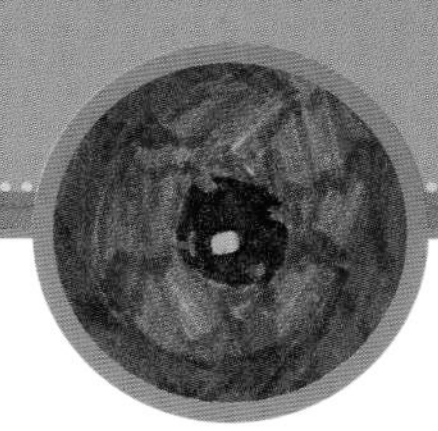

When my mom first got cancer, I had never heard of cancer before. I thought there might be something I could do to make it go away.

I felt

helpless.

Now that I'm older I know I can't make the cancer go away, but I can do things to help my mom like water the pansies.

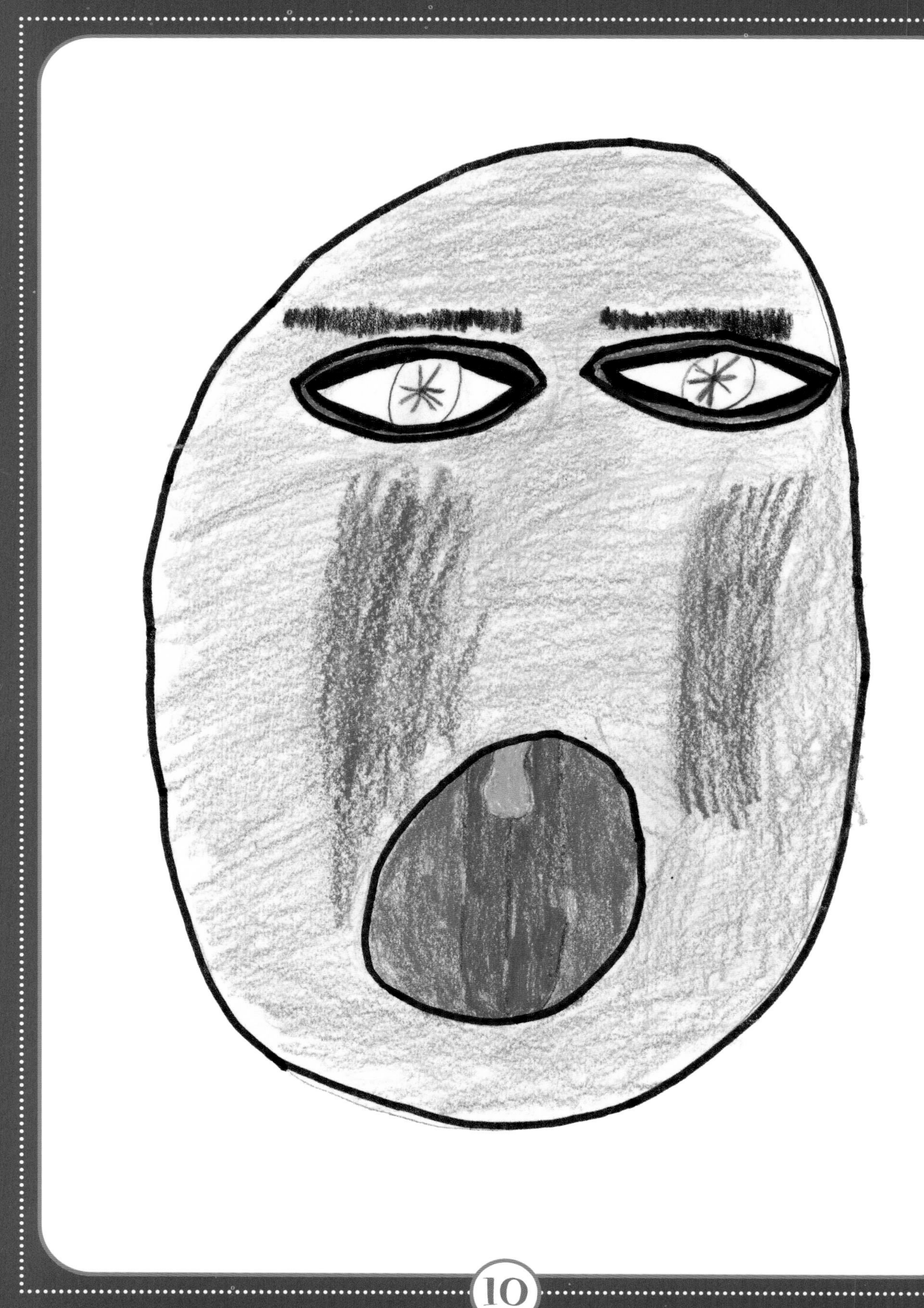

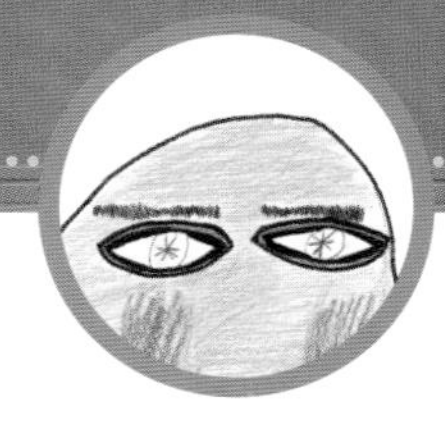

This is my

angry

picture.

Some days I am very mad about cancer.

This is my best tree painting ever.

One thing my mom tells me is that
I'm my own person.

She reminds me that my life is very full and
that her cancer is just one part of it.

That helps me feel

strong and sturdy

like this tree.

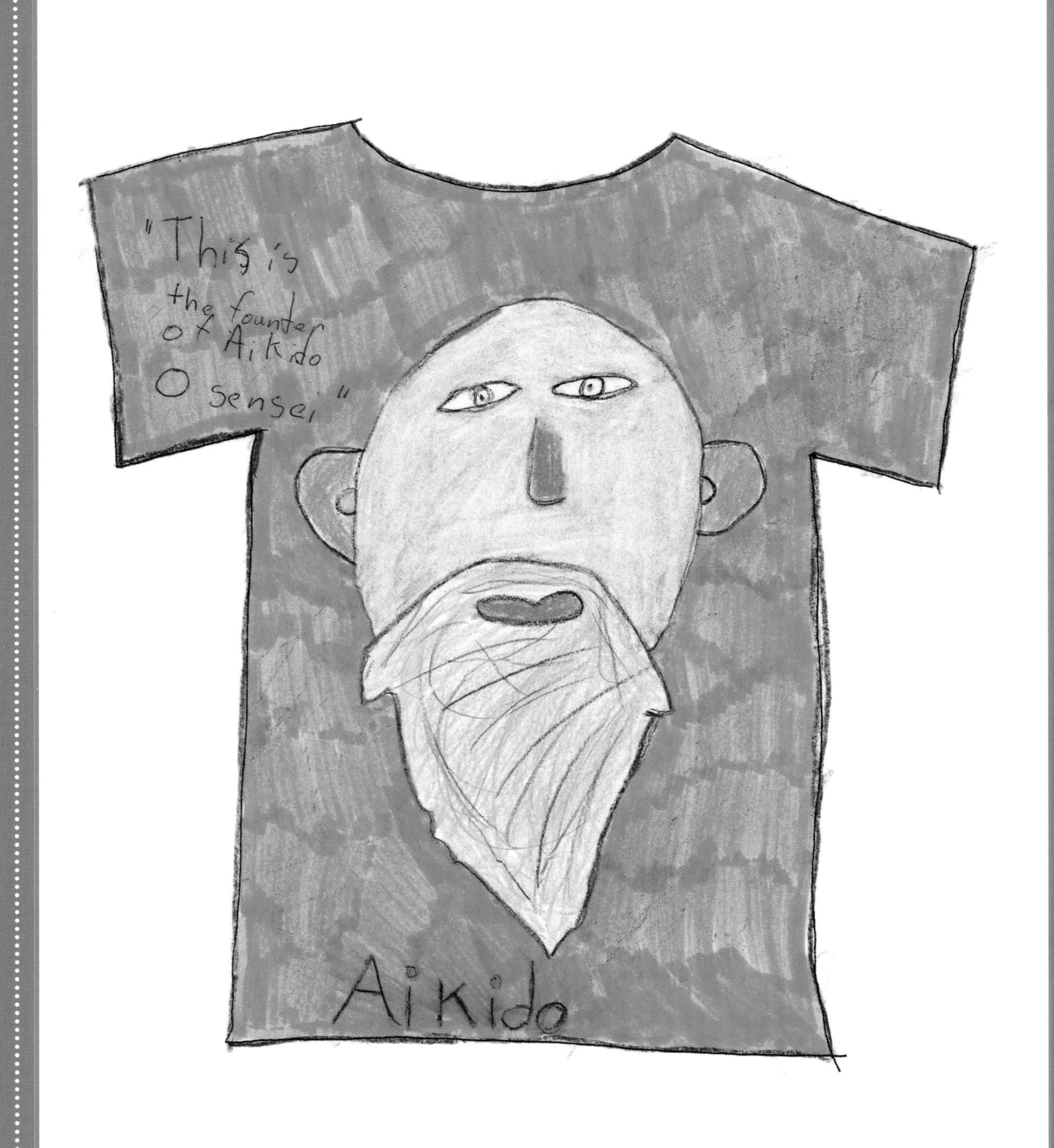
"This is
the founter
of Aikido
O sensei"
Aikido

I think the hardest thing for me is all the things my mom can't do that she used to do, like take me to Aikido and go to the movies.

The Doctor

My mom goes to lots of doctors.

One part of me likes them because
I want them to help my mom get better.

Another part feels like they get
to see my mom more than me.

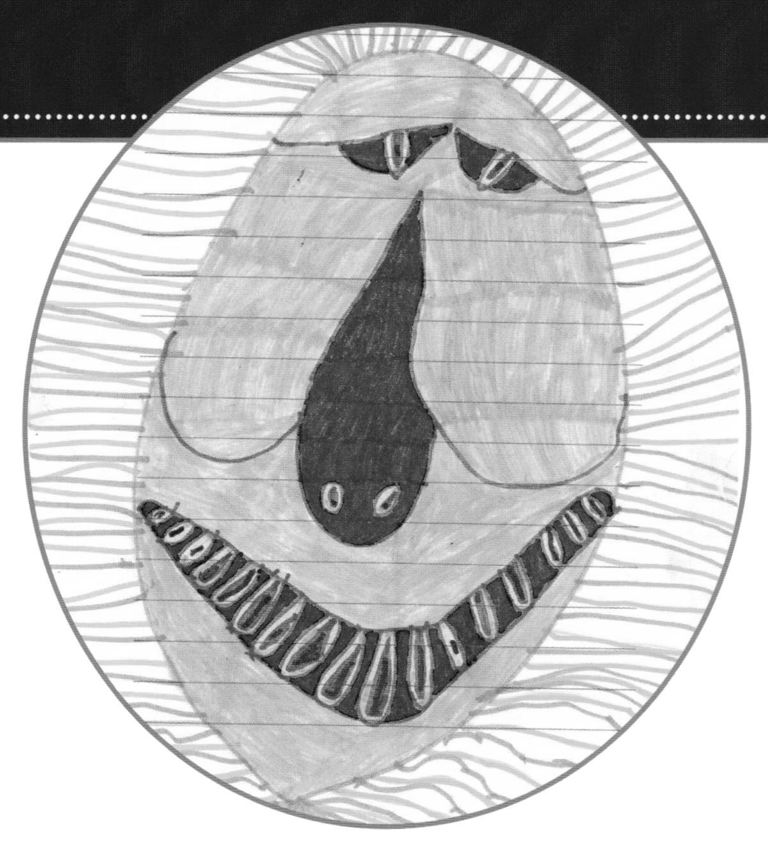

Shonook the Goblin

These are my two pictures about

scared.

As you can see one looks fierce
and one looks friendly.

One night my mom had to go the emergency room. That was very scary. It felt like Shonook was creeping around. I was very glad when mom came home even though I still get scared sometimes.

Sharmane the Unicorn

When mom snuggles me at night
she tells me stories of Sharmane.

They help me feel less scared and also

safe.

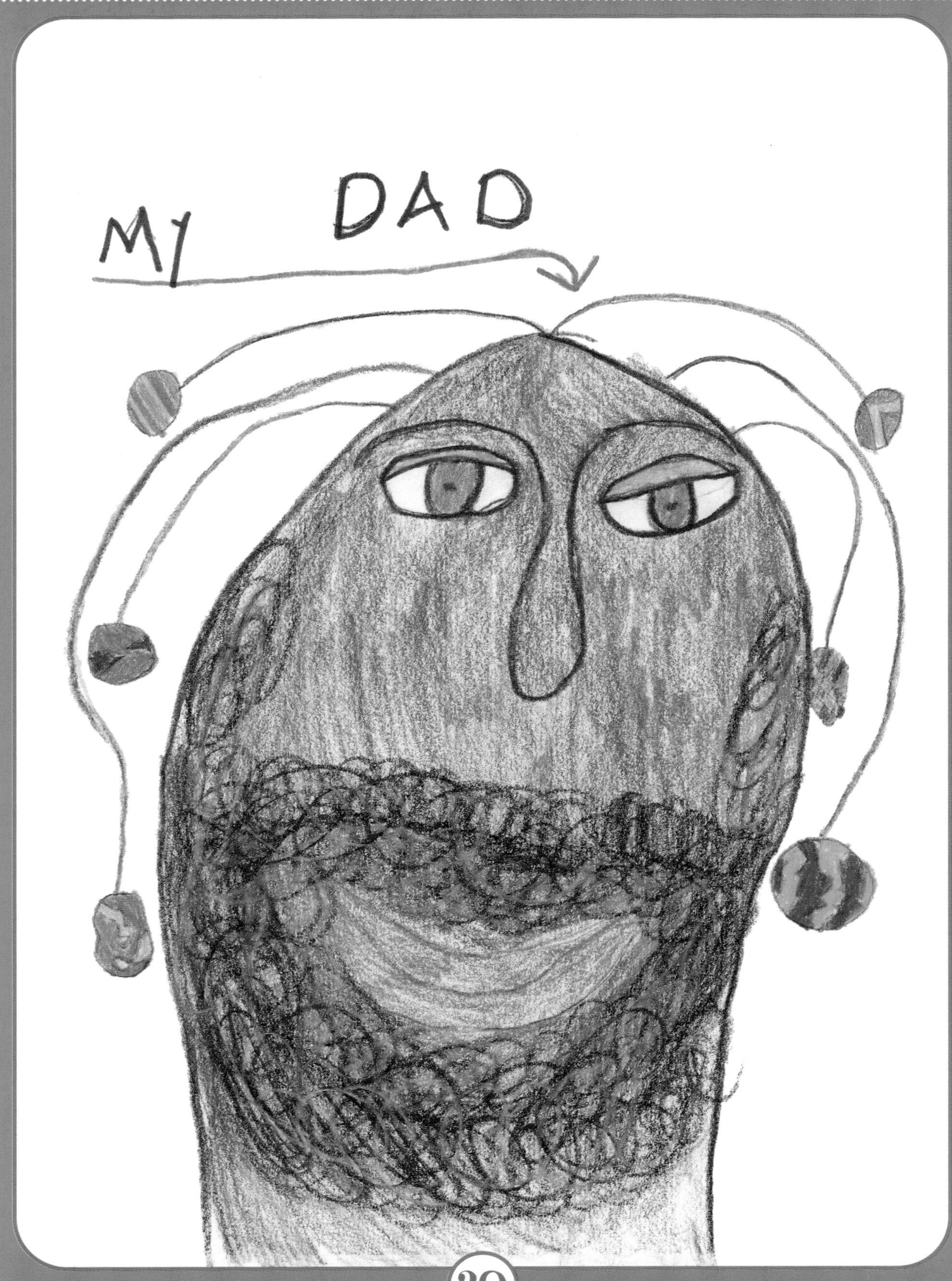
MY DAD

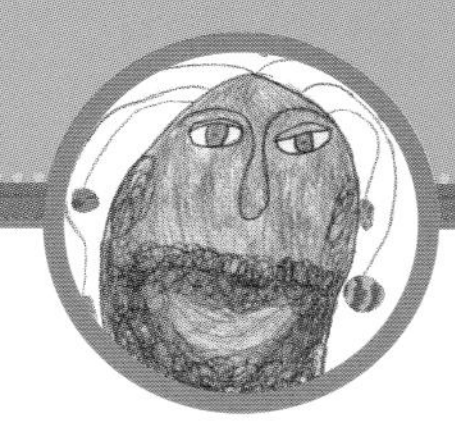

It's nice to have someone you can talk to.

It's also nice to have someone
who doesn't expect you to talk.

My dad is this person for me.

He knows how to listen.
He's someone I am
comfortable
with.

That's a very important thing.

My Mom's Feet

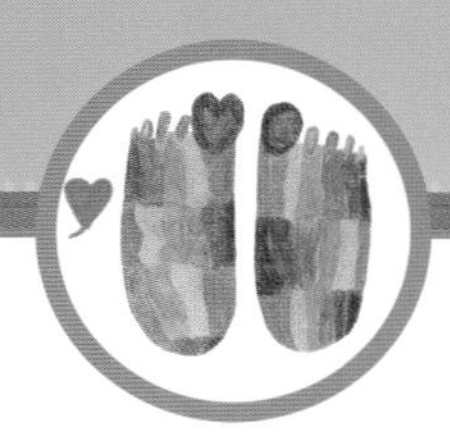

These are my mom's feet.
She loves to have her feet rubbed.

I always pour out gobs of massage
oil and that makes us laugh.

Mom reads to me while I rub her feet.

Mom says that

laughing

helps her immune system.

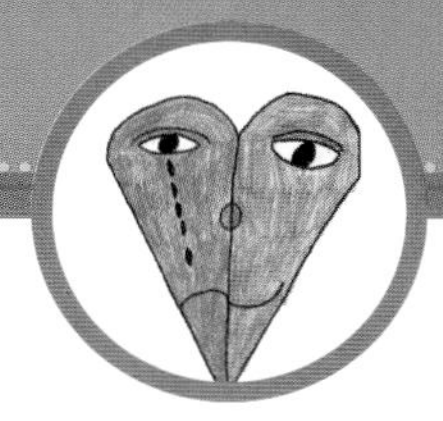

HAPPY

and

sad

at the same time.

This is my melting snowman.
My mom says he looks

I don't feel lonely because I have a loving family, but I bet some kids feel lonely when someone they love has cancer.

He's melting. That's good for the flower bulbs and spring grass. Some good things come out of cancer too. Those are harder to explain.

I call this

Sunny Day

because:

Mom felt good enough to
take me to my violin lesson.

The doctor said mom is doing better.

My sister did a very silly dance for me.

Self-portrait with red and white striped hair, age 10

I have a few more things to say about cancer.

I told my mom that maybe I used too many bright and happy colors. I don't want some other kids whose moms or dads or friends have cancer to think it is la-de-da.

Because cancer is no fun. But these are my favorite colors and also, even with my mom's cancer, I am

FOLLOW YOUR HEART

If you look closely at my picture which I drew one year ago you can see I have lots to love.

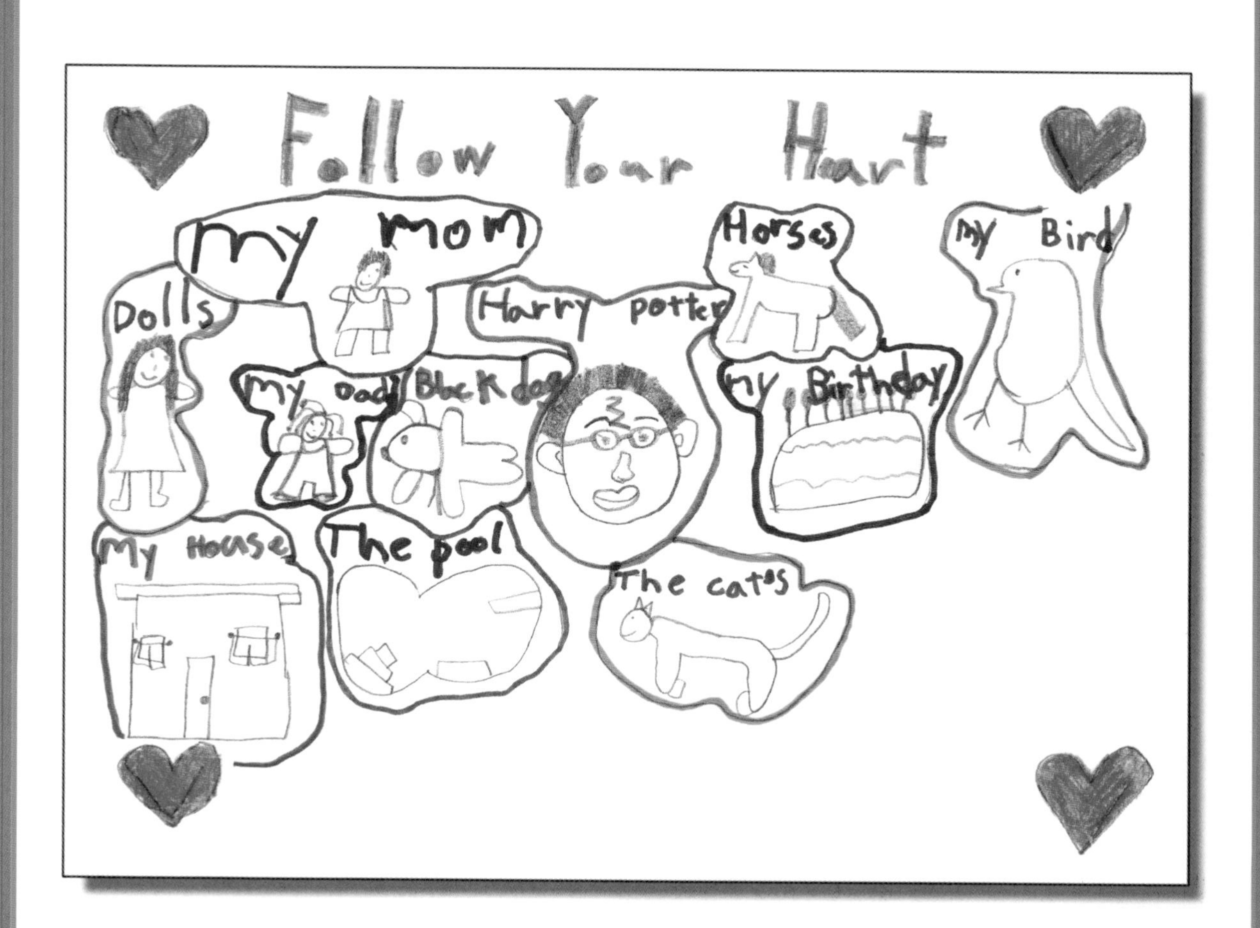

My mom and I wished on the same star.
Mom wished my wish to come true.

I wished the same wish I wish on every
candle, every fountain, and every star.

I bet you can guess what my wish is.

Here are some books you may find helpful.

For Children

Becky and the Worry Cup
by Wendy S. Harpham, M.D.
Perennial, 1997

Paper Chain
by Claire Blake
Health Press, 1998

You Are the Best Medicine
by Julie Agnier Clark
Balzer + Bray, 2010

For Adults

**When A Parent Has Cancer:
A Guide to Caring for Your Children**
by Wendy S. Harpham, M.D.
William Morrow Paperbacks, 2004

Writing Your Way Through Cancer
by Chia Martin
Hohm Press, 2000